Contents

KU-461-117

The world's energy sources

Today we use many different sources of energy. The energy powers machines and lights and heats our homes, schools, shops, offices and factories. We rely on many different fuels to drive cars, trains, ships and planes. We use various forms of energy to make electricity too. When you switch on a light or your computer, the energy to make them work might come from burning coal, flowing water or nuclear power.

Renewable or not

There are two basic groups of energy sources. One group includes the different forms of renewable energy. They are called renewable sources because they do not run out when they are used. Biomass, geothermal, solar, water and wind power are all renewable (and are described on pages 20-37). Fossil fuels – coal, oil and natural gas (see pages 8-15) – are called non-renewable because when they are used up, they cannot be replaced. The same is true of nuclear power (see pages 16-19), which depends on uranium, a metallic element that will one day run out.

What are the most pressing energy needs?

The International Energy Agency (IEA) and the United Nations Environment Programme (UNEP) say there are three urgent needs:

• ensuring continued access to energy supplies;

• reducing emissions of greenhouse gases;

• providing universal access to modern forms of energy.

The first need means avoiding an energy gap (see opposite). The IEA and UNEP say that poorer countries are especially at risk of having too few supplies. The second reason is just as important, because greenhouse gases are adding to the problems of global warming (see page 39).

As far as the third need goes, UNEP says that almost 1.6 million people in developing countries (about a quarter of the world's people) do not have electricity in their homes.

Where does our energy come from?

The chart shows the percentage of primary energy supplied by different energy sources.

1973   2005   2030

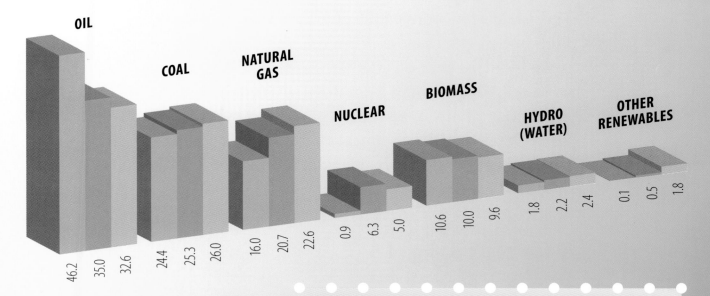

OIL
46.2 35.0 32.6

COAL
24.4 25.3 26.0

NATURAL GAS
16.0 20.7 22.6

NUCLEAR
0.9 6.3 5.0

BIOMASS
10.6 10.0 9.6

HYDRO (WATER)
1.8 2.2 2.4

OTHER RENEWABLES
0.1 0.5 1.8

Different shares

Today the three fossil fuels produce more than three quarters of our total energy, as the chart shows. The next biggest share comes from biomass (organic matter). The IEA forecasts that this situation is likely to stay the same for at least the next 20 years.

Avoiding an energy gap

We need to make the most of all our energy sources so we can make sure that we have enough energy in future. Towards the end of the twentieth century we became dependent on fossil fuels, but many countries have now agreed to use less coal, oil and gas. They want to do this because burning these fuels pollutes the atmosphere and adds to the greenhouse effect (see page 38). However, all national governments are aware that they need to supply enough energy for their citizens' needs. That's why they want to use energy from a variety of sources, including renewable sources.

Fossil fuels

The world's non-renewable energy sources are fossil fuels and nuclear power (from uranium). The main fossil fuels are coal, oil and natural gas. All three were originally formed from the fossilized remains of prehistoric plants or animals. They are all hydrocarbons – compounds of the chemical elements hydrogen and carbon – and they burn well in air and give off energy in the form of heat.

How oil and gas formed

Fossil fuels began to form more than three billion years ago. The world's early oceans were full of tiny, single-celled plants and animals, such as blue-green algae. When these microscopic organisms died, their remains sank to the seabed. They were soon covered by fine-grained mud and sand sediments, and over time the organic matter formed layers, as more dead plants and animals sank down on top. Each layer was then squashed by the weight of new layers above, and this process produced heat.

The combination of pressure and heat changed the sediments into rock such as sandstone (called sedimentary rock). At the same time the organic matter changed into a waxy substance called kerogen. This eventually separated into a liquid (oil) and a gas (natural gas).

Fuel from coal forests

Coal formed from larger, more complex plants that grew in swampy forests on land. Most coal began to form during the Carboniferous Period (or the Age of Coal Forests), which lasted from about 360

When will fossil fuels run out?

According to *World Factbook 2008*, we consume 80 million barrels of oil and 8300 cubic metres of gas a day. If we continue to use oil and gas at this rate and no more reserves are found, our current oil reserves would last for another 44 years (until 2052) and gas would last another 57 years (until 2065). Other experts estimate that we have enough gas to last for 72 years. As for coal, the World Coal Institute says: 'Coal reserves are available in almost every country worldwide, with recoverable reserves in around 70 countries. At current production levels, proven coal reserves are estimated to last 147 years [until 2155].'

to 286 million years ago. Giant ferns and other tree-like plants fell into the warm, shallow water of the swamps when they died. The dead vegetation on the forest floor was soon covered by more organic matter, so that layers were pressed tightly together.

Over a long period of time, pressure and heat changed the organic material into a spongy mass called peat. At the same time, other mineral matter turned into sedimentary rocks such as sandstone and shale. The increasing weight of the vegetable and mineral layers changed the peat into a drier, crumbly substance called lignite (from the Latin for wood), or brown coal. As the pressure increased, with more layers and greater depth, harder types of coal started to form.

Colourful layers of sandstone rocks in Malaysia. The layers build up pressure and heat.

Different types of coal

There are different types of coal. They were created by changes in pressure deeper underground, as layers built up over thousands and millions of years. Lignite eventually became sub-bituminous coal (from the Latin word *bitumen*, a kind of tarry pitch). As it became harder and drier, it turned into bituminous coal, and finally into the hardest coal of all, called anthracite (from the Greek word for coal). Coal miners dig out coal near the surface in opencast mines. They dig vertical shafts to reach the coal buried deep underground.

Coal around the world

The country which produces the most coal today is China. Coal was known there in ancient times, and China was probably the world's largest producer and consumer of coal until the seventeenth century. This changed during the Industrial Revolution in Europe and North America, when Britain and then America produced the most coal. By the beginning of this century China had become the biggest producer again, as you can see below.

Mining and the environment

One of the problems with coal (as well as other fossil fuels) is that mining can harm the environment. Opencast coalmines leave large areas of scarred land. Deep mines can cause land to subside so that it is dangerous for a long time after the mine is closed. Mine waste (called tailings) can pollute the environment, especially by seeping into waterways. Environmental groups are calling for governments to force mining companies to clean up the environment when they have finished mining in an area.

WORLD COAL PRODUCTION IN 2006

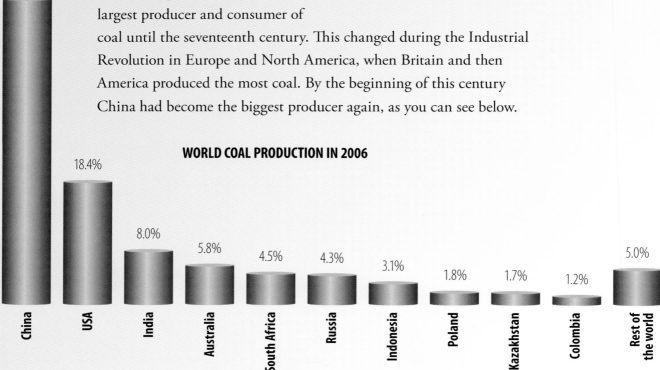

China 46.2%
USA 18.4%
India 8.0%
Australia 5.8%
South Africa 4.5%
Russia 4.3%
Indonesia 3.1%
Poland 1.8%
Kazakhstan 1.7%
Colombia 1.2%
Rest of the world 5.0%

A stock of fuel lies outside a coal-fired power station. A large plant burns more than 10,000 tonnes of coal a day to produce electricity.

Coal and electricity

The world's first coal-fired power station opened in 1882 in New York and the electricity it produced was used for lighting. Today, the US still produces half its electricity from coal, while China generates more than three quarters. Countries such as Australia, Poland and South Africa produce an even greater percentage of their energy from this source. Overall, coal makes up two fifths of the world's electricity generation. This is twice as much as gas, as you can see in the table.

Fuel used to generate electricity in 2005		
	Electricity %	Primary energy %
Coal	40	25
Natural gas	20	21
Oil	7	35
Total	**67**	**81**

Dirty versus clean coal

Environmentalists call coal 'dirty', because it releases polluting gases when it burns. But engineers are working on new methods to make it less polluting and are trying to produce what they call 'clean' coal. Coal can be treated so that it burns more efficiently. Putting the coal into a fluid allows unwanted material to sink so it can be removed. Another method is gasification, which turns the coal into gas. In a system called Integrated Gasification Combined Cycle (IGCC), coal reacts with oxygen and steam to form a 'syngas', which can be burned in a gas turbine. Waste gases given off when coal is burned can also be cleaned.

11

Black gold

Oil production did not start seriously until the middle of the nineteenth century. In 1859 a retired American railway conductor named Edwin Drake (1819-80) took over some oil pits in Pennsylvania. People had been drilling for oil there and elsewhere, but Drake had a new idea. As he drilled down using the power of a steam engine, he lined the drill hole with an iron pipe, so that it did not collapse and fill with earth or water. In this way Drake reached the bedrock at a depth of about 21 metres – and struck oil. Soon Drake and his men were filling old whiskey barrels with their 'black gold'.

A worker fuels an oil tanker in the Persian Gulf port of Dubai, in the United Arab Emirates.

Organizing petroleum

Much oil (or petroleum) is now produced in the Middle East. Oil was first discovered in the Persian desert (in present-day Iran) in 1890. Forty-six years later, prospectors found it on the other side of the Persian Gulf, in Saudi Arabia. The oil industry then grew throughout the region, and in 1960 four Middle Eastern countries – Iran, Iraq,

Kuwait and Saudi Arabia – joined with Venezuela to form the Organization of Petroleum Exporting Countries (OPEC). This organization now has 12 member countries and controls the price of oil sold by its members to oil companies around the world. Together, the OPEC countries produce 44 per cent of the world's oil.

Top ten oil countries

Ten countries produce two thirds of the world's oil and hold the same percentage of known reserves. Saudi Arabia is top of both lists.

	Kuwait	Venezuela	Norway	Canada	China	Mexico	Iran	USA	Russia	Saudi Arabia	Rest of the world
Production %	3.4	3.6	3.8	3.9	4.7	4.8	5.3	10.6	12.5	14.1	33.3
Reserves %	8.0	6.2	0.6	13.8	1.0	1.1	10.2	1.6	4.6	20.6	32.3

Why do oil prices matter?

The price of oil matters for several reasons. First, crude oil is refined into various mixtures of hydrocarbons. These include petrol (gasoline), diesel and similar fuels, which are burned to power cars, ships, planes and trains. When the cost of oil rises, the price of petrol and diesel goes up too. This matters to motorists and to transport companies. Second, oil is used to make many different products, including plastics, detergents, paints and synthetic fibres. When the oil price goes up, other prices rise too. Third, many financial experts believe that high oil prices slow down general economic growth around the world. Countries which import a lot of oil suffer when its price is high, while oil exporters do well at those times.

Rising prices

There was an oil crisis during the 1970s when the price of oil increased very fast. Since then the price has constantly changed, sometimes falling, but in recent years rising dramatically. This has made people nervous about relying on oil as an energy source. In 1999 the price of a barrel of oil fell to a low of US$16, but by 2004 it had reached $50. The price rose to $90 in 2007, and the following year it reached the level of $100 per barrel. This figure was widely publicized, and people around the world became aware that the price of petrol was rising rapidly.

What is natural gas?

Natural gas is composed mainly of methane, the lightest hydrocarbon, along with small amounts of ethane, propane, butane and pentane. These gases are dangerous to breathe in and, as natural gas has little or no smell, gas companies add a chemical to give it an odour. This means that people quickly notice leaks or gas coming from appliances which have been left on but not lit. We call it 'natural' gas to distinguish it from coal gas (or town gas), which is made from coal and was once more common.

Top ten gas countries

As with oil, ten countries produce two thirds of the world's oil and hold about the same percentage of known reserves.

	Saudi Arabia	Indonesia	Netherlands	Norway	UK	Algeria	Iran	Canada	USA	Russia	Rest of the world
Production %	2.4	2.6	2.7	2.9	3.0	3.0	3.6	6.3	17.3	23.2	33.0
Reserves %	8.0	6.2	0.6	1.3	0.3	3.1	15.4	0.9	3.2	27.8	33.2

The world's longest gas pipeline?

There are plans to build the longest pipeline in the world across more than 8000 kilometres of South American wilderness. The Gasoducto del Sur (Southern Gas Pipeline) would connect the gas fields of Venezuela to Argentina. But the pipeline would cross Brazil's Amazon rainforest, and environmentalists believe it could threaten both the natural habitat and local cultures. It could take up to 25 years to build the pipeline, once it has the official go-ahead.

Which fossil fuel is best for generating electricity?

The cheapest fuel is coal. That is why many governments continue to build coal-fired power stations, despite the problems of global warming (see page 39). As the US Department of Energy puts it: 'For the foreseeable future, coal will continue to be the dominant fuel used for electric power production. The low cost and abundance of coal is one of the primary reasons why consumers in the United States benefit from some of the lowest electricity rates of any free-market economy... While coal is the nation's major fuel for electric power, natural gas is the fastest growing fuel. More than 90 per cent of the power plants to be built in the next 20 years will likely be fueled by natural gas.' This may alter as the price of coal, natural gas and oil changes. Oil has become very expensive (see page 13), and most environmentalists agree that the best (or least damaging) fossil fuel is natural gas.

Russian gas

Russia tops both the production and reserves lists, and, together with Iran, has nearly half the world's known reserves. Many of Russia's gas fields are in the frozen northern region of Siberia. Long pipelines have been built so that Russia can export gas. The Trans-Siberian gas pipeline, first built in the 1980s, is 4500 kilometres long. It runs from the Urengoy gas field in Siberia to Ukraine and then to Western Europe. Another long pipeline runs from the Yamal peninsula in Siberia, through Belarus and Poland to Germany. A third is being built to the south east to deliver gas to China and Korea.

Building the Trans-Siberian pipeline was a huge feat of engineering. The pipe is 1.42 metres in diameter.

Nuclear power

Nuclear power comes from the energy inside atoms. The word nuclear refers to the nucleus, or central core, of an atom. When atomic nuclei are forced apart, a tremendous amount of energy is released. The same is true if atomic nuclei are forced together. Both processes are nuclear reactions: splitting is called fission, and joining fusion. Nuclear power plants around the world today use controlled nuclear fission to produce energy that is turned into electricity.

Nuclear fuel and waste

The nuclear fuel cycle is a series of linked processes that produce electricity in nuclear reactors. The cycle begins with mining uranium ore, which is processed and then used as nuclear fuel. After it has produced electricity, some of the spent fuel is reprocessed so that it can go back to a reactor and begin the cycle all over again. Fuel that cannot be reprocessed is waste and this presents the nuclear power industry with a huge problem, because the waste is dangerously radioactive and can remain so for hundreds of years.

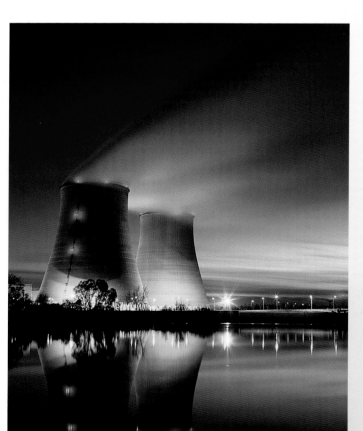

Cooling towers at the nuclear power station at Belleville in central France. Two nuclear reactors have been producing electricity at the plant since 1988.

Atomic research

The German-born physicist Albert Einstein (1879-1955) worked out that the mass (or amount of matter) in atoms can change into energy. He also created a formula for calculating the amount of atomic energy released. This was the famous equation $E = mc^2$, showing that energy (E) equals mass (m) multiplied by the speed of light (c) multiplied by itself (^{2}). His work showed that the energy released by atomic changes, such as splitting a nucleus, is enormous. Scientists later worked out that splitting one kilogram of uranium releases the same energy as 16 million kilograms of high explosive (TNT).

Top nuclear producers

The United States produces more nuclear-generated electricity than any other country – nearly a third of the world total. The second biggest producer is France, which generates more than three quarters of its electricity in nuclear reactors.

Number of reactors

% of world nuclear power

% of national electricity

Country	Number of reactors	% of world nuclear power	% of national electricity
USA	104	30.9	19.4
France	59	16.1	76.9
Japan	55	10.2	27.5
Russia	31	5.7	16.0
South Korea	20	5.2	35.3
Germany	17	5.1	25.9
Canada	18	3.7	14.7
Ukraine	15	3.4	48.1
Sweden	10	2.5	46.1
China	11	2.3	1.9
Rest of the world	99	14.9	

What happens to nuclear waste?

Used fuel is cooled in storage pools near the reactor. It is then prepared for permanent disposal or reprocessing. There are major reprocessing plants in France, Russia and the UK, which deal with about 5000 tonnes of used fuel per year. There are no long-term storage facilities yet for the rest, but experts believe it is best to bury it deep underground. The USA is planning a long-term storage site at Yucca Mountain in Nevada. The World Nuclear Association says that about 270,000 tonnes of spent fuel are stored around the world, mostly at reactor sites. About 12,000 tonnes are added yearly of which 3000 tonnes go for reprocessing.

Nuclear-powered electricity

The method of generating electricity inside power plants is basically the same for all fossil fuels and uranium. The only difference is that coal, oil and gas are burned to release energy, while uranium undergoes nuclear fission. This happens inside a reactor, where the nuclei of a form of uranium called U-235 are split. A nuclear chain reaction – when the fission process repeats itself over and over again – is carefully controlled, so that energy is released slowly. The split nuclei give off energy as heat, which is used to boil water and produce steam. The pressurized steam drives the blades of a turbine, and the shaft of the turbine is connected to an electric generator.

Weapons of mass destruction

Many people dislike the idea of using nuclear power because they fear a link with nuclear weapons. The energy and military uses are similar, but weapons-grade uranium is quite different and in a nuclear weapon chain reactions are allowed to go totally out of control. Few countries in the world have nuclear weapons. According to the Carnegie Endowment for International Peace, in 2007 the estimated numbers of nuclear warheads were as shown on the right.

Russia	16,000
USA	10,300
China	410
France	350
UK	200
Israel	100-170
India	75-110
Pakistan	50-110
Total	**~ 27,600**

The International Atomic Energy Agency

The IAEA helps to overcome many of the world's safety concerns. The agency promotes the peaceful use of nuclear energy and tries to reduce its use for military purposes. Newspapers sometimes call the IAEA the United Nations' nuclear watchdog. The agency was founded in 1957 and its headquarters are in Vienna, Austria.

Safety concerns

There are safety concerns about all methods of energy production, and safety is a major issue when it comes to nuclear power. There are several reasons for this. The first is the possibility of an accident at a reactor. This would be much more catastrophic than an accident at other power plants.

The worst nuclear accident there has ever been was at Chernobyl in Ukraine, in 1986. A sudden, uncontrolled power surge caused a steam explosion. This blew the lid off one of the Soviet plant's reactors and damaged the containment building. The explosion caused a fire and threw particles of nuclear fuel and radioactive elements up into the air in a swirling cloud. The radioactive plume soon spread over a wide area, and fallout reached parts of Belarus, Moldova and Russia. Levels of radioactivity rose as far away as Britain and Ireland. Scientists have estimated that the disaster released a hundred times more radiation than the two atom bombs dropped on Hiroshima and Nagasaki in 1945.

Nuclear travel

Nuclear reactors need no air and use very little enriched U-235 as fuel. They can be used to drive ships and submarines. The reactor produces steam to drive a turbine and turn a propeller shaft. A nuclear submarine can stay underwater for a long time without needing to refuel. The first nuclear sub, the *USS Nautilus*, was launched in 1954, and four years later it reached the North Pole beneath the frozen surface of the Arctic Ocean.

The 97.5-metre long USS Nautilus *enters New York Harbor in 1957. The submarine was in operation until 1979.*

Never-ending energy

There are five main sources of renewable energy –
biomass, geothermal, solar, water and wind power.
They are all becoming more important, as people realize
that they are much less polluting than fossil fuels and
have less effect on global warming (see page 39).

Despite this, the International Energy Agency (IEA) expects
only a small increase in the use of renewable energy by 2030. Experts
forecast that about one seventh of our energy needs will be met from
renewables. If governments follow the agency's suggested energy policies,
renewable sources might make up one sixth of the total (compared
with nearly one third for oil and about one fifth each for coal and gas).
The IEA forecasts that electricity produced from renewable sources will
increase by 2030 to at least one fifth of the total.

	1973	2005	2030
Coal	38.3	40.3	37.6
Natural gas	12.1	19.7	28.7
Oil	24.7	6.6	4.0
Nuclear	3.3	15.2	9.6
Water	21.0	16.0	13.9
Other renewables	0.6	2.2	6.2

The power of moving water

Since ancient times, people have found ways of using the flow of
rivers and streams to turn wheels that operate machinery. Waterwheels
developed into hydroelectric power plants that generate vast amounts
of electricity today. More recently, engineers have developed ways to
harness the power of ocean waves, tides and currents. They have even

The ultimate energy source

All our energy comes from the Sun, making it the ultimate energy source. Solar power is direct energy from the Sun. The power of moving air (wind) and moving water (in rivers and oceans) is created by Earth's weather patterns, which are themselves produced by solar heat. The Sun is also the source of geothermal energy (heat from inside the Earth), because planet Earth would never have formed (and would never have been hot) if its original material had not been sent spinning around a star – the Sun. All the living plants and animals that make up biomass also rely on the Sun for their energy. Since fossil fuels are prehistoric biomass, they too were formed from the power of the Sun – our ultimate energy source.

found a way of using the temperature difference between deep and surface water to drive turbines.

Hydroelectric dams

A hydroelectric dam across a river slows the natural flow of water and creates a reservoir. This helps to produce electricity by ensuring that there is always a large store of water ready for use. Dams have channels, called penstocks, below the waterline of the reservoir. Water flows down each penstock by the force of gravity. As it flows through the channel, the water turns the blades of a turbine. This changes the kinetic energy of the water (produced by movement) into mechanical energy which can power a machine. The blades are connected to a shaft, which turns an electric generator. The dam's turbines are kept turning by the huge volumes of water stored in the reservoir.

The Itaipu dam lies on the Paraná River, which forms the border between Brazil and Paraguay. The dam has been generating electricity since 1984.

Top ten hydropower producers

China generates more hydroelectricity than any other country, but this is less than a sixth of the electric power it uses altogether. There are vast Chinese hydroelectric schemes, but coal still produces much more power. Number two in the list, Canada, generates more than half its electricity by water power, and the third biggest producer – Brazil – generates more than three quarters. In Norway, hydroelectric dams produce nearly all the country's electricity.

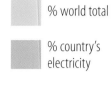

% world total

% country's electricity

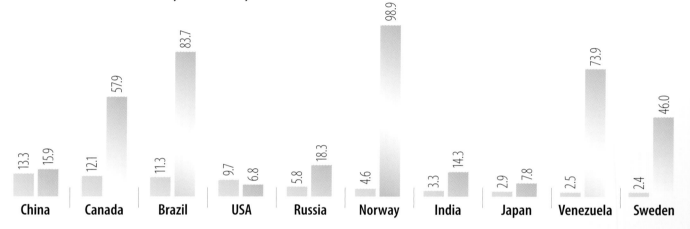

China	Canada	Brazil	USA	Russia	Norway	India	Japan	Venezuela	Sweden
13.3 / 15.9	12.1 / 57.9	11.3 / 83.7	9.7 / 6.8	5.8 / 18.3	4.6 / 98.9	3.3 / 14.3	2.9 / 7.8	2.5 / 73.9	2.4 / 46.0

Biggest hydroelectric project

The most powerful hydroelectric project in the world is being built on the Chang Jiang, China's longest river. Building work on the concrete dam began in 1993, and the project should be complete by 2011. This enormous power plant will bring electricity to millions of Chinese villagers for the first time, generating more than 22,000 megawatts from 26 generators. The wall of the dam is 185 metres high and more than two kilometres long and it has created an enormous 660-kilometre long reservoir. China has many more hydroelectric schemes planned. It wants to nearly triple its hydropower capacity by 2020, when it aims to produce 15 per cent of its energy from renewable sources.

Micro-hydro systems

In regions where there is no national electricity grid, especially in developing countries, small-scale schemes are becoming increasingly popular. Micro-hydro schemes can produce enough power for small communities from

China's Three Gorges Dam under construction. This huge project has caused a great deal of controversy. The dam has been heavily criticized by environmentalists.

rivers and streams. They work by allowing fast-flowing water to turn the blades of a small turbine. In recent years, this form of hydropower has been growing at about eight per cent per year worldwide.

One of the great advantages of micro-hydro power is that electricity can be produced very close to where it is used. This means that there is no need for transmission pylons and so the systems have little effect on the environment. Micro-hydro schemes are very useful in mountainous regions, where streams run fast all year round. They are becoming very important in countries such as Bhutan and Nepal in the Himalayas, and on the island of Sri Lanka. In China, micro-hydro schemes are also multiplying fast.

Are hydro schemes bad for the environment?

They do have great impact on the environment. Hydroelectric dams and reservoirs can cause landslides, soil erosion and water pollution. The Three Gorges Dam has had a huge impact on the local population, and as many as two million people have had to move home because they lived on land that was to be flooded. In 2007, the Chinese state media announced that a further four million people would have to move because of the possibility of the dam causing 'an environmental catastrophe'. The build-up of silt in the reservoir will reduce the amount of silt carried downstream and this could cause more erosion and sinking of land in coastal areas. The Chinese government has said that the dam will help to control floods along the Chang Jiang, but some environmentalists doubt this. They also point out that hydro projects can be unreliable during long dry seasons and droughts.

Tidal energy

Hundreds of years ago, tide mills operated along the Atlantic coasts of Europe and North America. Their waterwheels used the power of ocean tides rather than the fast-flowing water of a river. Seawater flowed into a pond as the tide came in and the water level rose. After the tide had gone out again, the pond's water was released through a sluice and turned a waterwheel. Today, three different methods are being used to harness tidal energy. They all use turbines beneath the surface of the water. The first method involves building a barrage across a tidal estuary. The second creates an offshore tidal lagoon and the third uses tidal streams or currents.

Barrage technology

Tidal barrages work in a similar way to hydroelectric dams. The barrage is a long concrete barrier built across a wide estuary at the mouth of a river. The river water upstream of the barrage, called the basin, acts like a reservoir. The barrage has sluices which let water though, and a series of turbines that power generators. At low tide, the sluices are left open. As the tide comes in and water flows from the ocean into the estuary, the water level rises and the basin fills up. Then the sluice gates are closed until the tide has gone out again. As the sea level falls, it creates a drop between the basin and the sea. Then the turbine gates are opened so that ebbing water flows through them.

Past and future projects

A 333-metre long barrage on the River Rance, in northern France, became the world's first working tidal power plant in 1966. Its 24 turbines produce 240 megawatts of electricity – just over one per cent of the electricity produced by the Three Gorges Dam. In the UK, there are plans to build a tidal barrage across the Severn Estuary, which has one of the largest tidal ranges in the world (an average of about 13 metres

What is a watt?

A watt (W) is a unit of power, which measures the rate of producing or using energy. The term was named after the Scottish engineer James Watt (1736-1819), who developed an improved steam engine. Watt himself measured his engine's performance in horsepower (hp). One horsepower equals 746 watts. Today, watts are generally used to measure electric power.

1 kilowatt (kW) = 1 thousand watts

1 megawatt (MW) = 1 million watts

1 gigawatt (GW) = 1 thousand million watts

This Danish wave-energy device is a Wave Dragon. The power of waves pushes seawater into a reservoir. The water is let out again through turbines that drive an electric generator. The dragon is an overtopping device.

between high and low tide). The idea is to build a 16-kilometre long barrage with 200-300 turbines. This would generate more than 8000 MW of electricity (at least 33 times more than the Rance barrage), providing nearly five per cent of the UK's electricity in 11 years' time.

Wave farms

Another exciting development is different kinds of wave farms. These are based on floating devices that are moored out to sea and move with the waves. The movement drives generators and creates electricity. One wave generator is shaped like a sea snake, while others are types of buoys. There is even a land-based system, which uses the power of waves as they hit the shore.

The environmental case for barrages

Many environmentalists like this technology because it does not produce greenhouse gases, apart from in the construction of the barrage. However, there could be huge effects on the nearby coastline, and especially the intertidal habitat (the coastal area that is covered at high tide and exposed at low tide). Rivers and estuaries carry a large amount of sediment to the sea, and barrages can affect this, leading to a build-up of sediment within the basin. In turn, these changes have a big impact on local wildlife.

Wind-powered wheels

The wind is another powerful force caused by our planet's weather. People have used wind for centuries to drive windmills. Many of these were used by millers to grind grain and make flour. The Netherlands is famous for its old windmills, but these were used to pump water rather than for milling. Dutch people have been using wind power to drain their low-lying, flat land since the fifteenth century. In present-day America, wind pumps are still used to draw up underground water for livestock. They are also useful in arid African countries for filling up waterholes.

Developing wind-powered electricity

Today, modern wind turbines are used to produce electricity. This idea began in 1888, when an American inventor named Charles Brush decided to try a new system for generating electricity. He had been using a horse-drawn treadmill to power a simple generator, but he replaced the animals with a 17-metre wind-wheel in the garden of his mansion. The wheel drove a dynamo that produced 12 kilowatts of electricity and lit 350 lights.

Workers inspect and clean a turbine cover at a wind-turbine plant in Urumqi, China. The turbines could be used at the Dabancheng wind farm (see page 29).

Part of the Burbo Bank offshore wind farm in Liverpool Bay, England. The wind farm, which opened in 2007, has 25 turbines and generates 90 MW.

Modern wind turbines

The most common kind of turbine (or aerogenerator) today is the three-blade horizontal axis wind turbine (or HAWT for short). This has proved to be the most efficient design for large wind turbines with a rotor diameter of 40–90 metres. Using three blades makes the rotation smoother and is believed to be calmer on the eye than two or four or more blades. Turbines have become larger and larger in recent years, and today the tallest are more than 100 metres high. One of the latest German wind turbines is 135 metres high at the hub and has a rotor diameter of 126 metres.

Wind farms

Individual wind turbines do not produce enormous amounts of electricity compared with power stations fired by fossil fuels. A turbine may produce just one MW of power, though the biggest are six or seven times more powerful. A large coal-fired power station can produce 5000 MW, which is why energy companies put wind turbines in big groups called wind farms (or parks). They are often sited on land, but sometimes offshore.

Do millers still use old windmills?

Some old windmills have been renovated and still produce stoneground flour. Outwood post mill in Surrey was built in 1665 and is the oldest working windmill in the UK. However, most millers find that wind is less efficient and powerful than other sources of energy. James Watt built the first steam-powered flour mill in 1780, and during the twentieth century steam was overtaken by electricity. Today, flour is generally milled between electrically-powered steel rollers rather than wind-powered stones.

Windy world

According to the World Wind Energy Association, wind produces electricity in more than 70 countries. The amount of electricity produced has been growing by more than 25 per cent a year in recent times. In 2007, wind produced 1.3 per cent of the electricity used in the world. As the chart (right) shows, the four leading wind-energy countries together produce two thirds of the world's wind power.

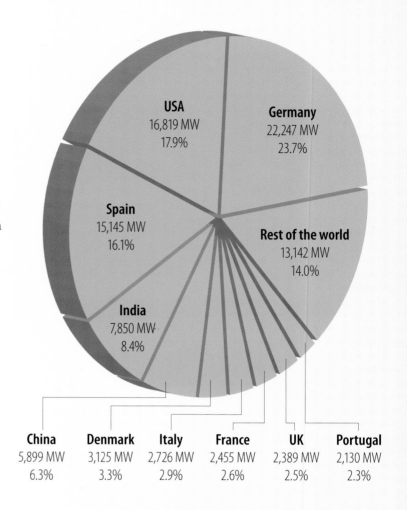

USA
16,819 MW
17.9%

Germany
22,247 MW
23.7%

Spain
15,145 MW
16.1%

Rest of the world
13,142 MW
14.0%

India
7,850 MW
8.4%

China
5,899 MW
6.3%

Denmark
3,125 MW
3.3%

Italy
2,726 MW
2.9%

France
2,455 MW
2.6%

UK
2,389 MW
2.5%

Portugal
2,130 MW
2.3%

Three Gorges of the sky

Hydropower is increasingly important in China (see page 22). Wind power is increasing in importance, too. Experts predict that China's wind-generated power could make up to ten per cent of the country's electricity by 2020. By then wind turbines could produce five times the amount of electricity generated by their largest hydroelectric

The world's largest wind farm

The world's largest wind farm is the Horse Hollow Wind Energy Center near Abilene, Texas. Covering 240 square kilometres, the centre has more than 400 80-metre turbines. Together they produce 735 megawatts of electricity.

plant. At Dabancheng, in Xinjiang province in the north-west of the country, they are building a wind farm that could one day be the biggest in the world. Chinese wind engineers are calling it the 'Three Gorges of the sky' after the dam.

Farming ocean winds

The surface of the ocean is much smoother than land, so average wind speed over open water is usually much higher. This means that offshore wind farms can be more efficient and powerful than onshore parks. Turbines are easiest to put up in shallow waters, because their foundations have to be built on the seabed. Countries with long coastlines and shallow continental shelves – such as Denmark and the UK – offer many good locations for offshore wind farms.

Small wind

Wind power can be produced on a small scale for individual homes, businesses or small communities. In the industrialized world, this is becoming a popular way for environmentally conscious people to generate their own electricity. They can have a small turbine put up on their roof. One of the most successful markets for 'small wind' is the United States, where the use of small turbines is growing by nearly a fifth every year.

'Not in my back yard!'

One of the problems with all electricity production is that people do not want unsightly technology to be visible from their homes. This is known as the NIMBY attitude (standing for Not In My Back Yard). Most people are happy to have wind farms or other kinds of power stations, because they want a secure and plentiful supply of electricity. But they usually want them somewhere else. Are wind turbines really a blot on the landscape? Many people believe so and are violently opposed to wind farms. But others see turbines as environmentally sound technology and find them positively attractive. What do you think? Do you like the look of wind turbines? If you do, would you want one near your house?

Biomass – the world of living things

Scientists call all organic matter (or living things) biomass. The term comes from the Greek word *bios* (meaning life) and mass (meaning quantity of matter). Today, we also use the term biomass to mean organic matter that can be used as a source of energy. For thousands of years people have burned wood and other plants as fuels, to provide heat for warmth and cooking.

In more recent times, we have found ways to use biomass as an energy source to power machines and produce electricity. When we burn biomass, carbon goes back into the atmosphere as carbon dioxide. This speeds up a natural process, which happens anyway when plants or animals die. If we make sure that the biomass used is replaced by newly planted material (which will take in CO_2), the fuel use is considered to be carbon neutral. It is called neutral because using it does not add to the amount of carbon circulating in the natural cycle, but it does not take away from it either.

Traditional biomass

Today, energy experts refer to firewood (or fuelwood) as traditional biomass. Modern biomass energy involves converting biomass into biofuels, gas and electricity. Experts estimate that ten per cent of world energy for cooking and heating comes from traditional biomass and that this is used by more than a third of the world's people. In Africa, nearly three quarters of the population rely on firewood.

The second generation

Many experts believe that we are moving into the age of second-generation biofuels. These are made from the non-food parts of plants, such as stalks, stems, leaves and husks, which are usually left as waste once seeds and other edible parts have been removed. Second-generation crops also include non-food plants (such as switchgrass and sunflowers) and industry waste, such as fruit skins. The resulting biofuel is often called cellulosic ethanol (from cellulose, which makes up the cell walls of plants).

Biofuels

Liquid biofuels can power cars. They have been developed from different plants in various parts of the world. In Europe, biofuels are mainly made from rape (a plant of the cabbage family with oil-bearing seeds), wheat and sugar beet. In North America, maize (corn) and soya beans are common sources, while in South America sugar cane is grown for the purpose. In Southeast Asian countries, oil palms are the main source of biofuels.

Ethanol

Ethanol (or ethyl alcohol) is a kind of alcohol that can be mass-produced by fermenting plants. This means breaking down the sugar or starch in plants by the action of microorganisms, such as those in yeast. The United States and Brazil produced more than four fifths of the world's ethanol in 2007. Brazilian manufacturers use sugar cane as their source, while 98 per cent of US ethanol is made from maize. The illustration on the right shows the top five countries' ethanol production as a percentage of the world total.

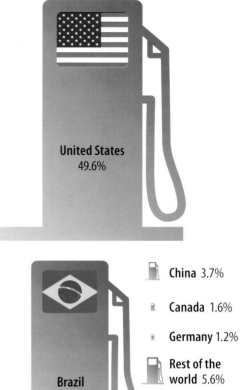

United States
49.6%

Brazil
38.3%

China 3.7%

Canada 1.6%

Germany 1.2%

Rest of the world 5.6%

Ethanol is produced from sugar cane at a plant in São Tomé, Brazil.

Rising food prices

According to a report by the Food and Agriculture Organization (FAO) of the United Nations, widespread hunger in the world is being made worse by a global rise in food prices. Experts say prices are being driven up because plants are being used to produce biofuels. They believe the demand for fuel in rich countries is competing with the need for food in poor countries. In 2008 the FAO said that 37 of the world's poorer countries were suffering from food crises and large numbers of their people simply did not have enough to eat.

Food versus fuel

Experts have worked out that the quantity of grain (maize or corn) needed to produce ethanol to fill the 90-litre fuel tank of a four-wheel-drive vehicle would be enough to feed one person for a whole year. For this reason, many people see biofuels as a bad thing because they are based on foodstuffs. The development of non-food biofuel is vitally important. But this still leaves the question of farmers and businessmen concentrating on crops for fuel rather than food. In 2007 an important member of the United Nations' staff called the trade in biofuel 'a crime against humanity' and proposed a five-year ban on biofuel production.

American food aid is unloaded from a cargo ship in Somalia, East Africa.

Dealing with deforestation

Another problem caused by increased demand for biofuels is deforestation (cutting down trees and destroying forests). In Malaysia many forests are being destroyed to satisfy the demand for biofuels from palm oil. On the islands of Sumatra and Borneo, four million hectares of forest have been replaced with palm farms. A further 22 million hectares are due to be cleared. Environmentalists are concerned about deforestation, because it adds to the effects of global warming (see page 39).

Power from waste

Biomass power can also be developed from all kinds of organic waste matter. Most people agree that using the rotting material in our waste dumps and huge landfill sites is a good thing. One particular benefit is that this is waste food rather than edible food.

Third-generation biofuels

A third generation of biofuels may be just around the corner. This biofuel will be based on algae. These simple organisms are similar to plants and live mainly in water. The best known examples of algae are different kinds of seaweed. Researchers are working on ways to produce biofuel from algae collected from ponds, lakes, rivers and even sewage farms. They say it is possible to produce more than 100,000 litres of ethanol a year from one hectare of algae. This is 13 times more productive than sugar cane and 16 times more than palm oil. Biomass companies are calling this biofuel green crude (referring to crude oil).

Gobar gas

Gobar is the Hindi word for cow dung, so it is easy to work out where gobar gas comes from. There are many gobar gas plants in India and Pakistan. A gobar digester plant is a round concrete pit built near cattle sheds.

Power from above and below

The Sun is our ultimate energy source (see page 21). Inside the Sun, which is the nearest star to Earth, nuclear reactions give off energy and create enormous heat. This happens as the nuclei of atoms of hydrogen – the lightest of all gases – join together to form the nucleus of a heavier gas, called helium. The Sun gives off most of this energy in the form of electromagnetic radiation (electrical and magnetic waves).

Electromagnetic radiation includes radio waves, microwaves, infrared rays, visible radiation (light), ultraviolet rays, X rays and gamma rays. Nearly half the Sun's electromagnetic radiation is in the form of infrared rays, which we feel on Earth as heat. Most of the other half is the visible radiation – or sunlight – to which our eyes are sensitive.

Solar panels for heating

One of the best ways to make direct use of the Sun's energy is to include solar panels as part of a hot-water system. The flat panels are usually positioned on a roof, facing the right direction (south in the northern hemisphere) and tilted at an angle which collects as much sunshine as possible. Each panel has a series of narrow pipes running through it. These are warmed by the Sun's heat, which is then absorbed by the water or other liquid inside them.

Saharan sunshine

Researchers are looking at the northern regions of the Sahara Desert. They say that solar power plants there could generate all the electricity needed by Europe, the Middle East and North Africa. The scheme would use less than 0.3 per cent of the desert areas of that region.

Photovoltaic cells

The term photovoltaic comes from photo (meaning light) and volt (a unit of electrical force). So photovoltaic power means electrical power from light. Photovoltaic (or PV) systems convert solar energy into electricity, using sunlight to power electrical equipment. PV (or solar) cells were first made

These reflecting dishes in New South Wales, Australia, concentrate the Sun's rays to a spot where they can boil water. The resulting steam is used to create electricity.

in the nineteenth century, but they were not very efficient until the 1950s. They work by the movement of electrons, which are particles that occur in atoms.

Electric power plants

Solar energy can power large-scale electricity plants when big banks of PV cells are put next to each other. But the future lies with concentrating solar power (CSP) systems. One CSP system uses reflecting dishes (parabolic reflectors), which concentrate sunlight on to a receiver containing a fluid that is heated. The receiver contains a heat engine that generates electricity.

Are solar cars and other vehicles practical?

The first solar-powered car was developed in 1982. By 2005 the World Solar Challenge race had been won by a solar car travelling at more than 100 km/h. But solar cars are not yet practical. The group of PV cells takes up a large area, which is difficult to design into an ordinary road car. Also, a solar car needs a very large battery. Solar-powered boats and planes also need more work and research. At the moment solar vehicles are adventurous experiments, but that is exactly how many technological developments started out.

Steam pipes at one of the Geysers geothermal power plants in California, USA.

Underground heat

The origins of geothermal energy are deep inside the Earth. The word geothermal comes from the Greek words *ge* (meaning Earth) and *therme* (heat), and the energy is produced by our planet's natural heat. This comes from deep inside the Earth, where the core of the planet is hotter than the surface of the Sun.

Beneath the Earth's solid crust (outer surface layer) there is a thick layer of molten rock. This hot rock (called magma) comes to the surface through cracks in the crust and creates volcanoes. In places where magma comes close to the surface, we can harness geothermal heat and use it as a power source.

Italian hot springs and steam

The ancient Romans realized that they could use the water from hot springs (underground water heated by magma) for their bathing houses. Early in the twentieth century, engineers in Italy used steam coming from underground to drive a simple generator and produce electricity.

Direct use

We can use hot water from geothermal springs in heating systems. This is called a direct use of geothermal power. The thermal water circulates through pipes, just as heated water does in a central heating system fired by another fuel, such as oil or natural gas. Or the thermal water can heat cold water that serves the same purpose. The best example of direct use is Iceland, where geothermal power is used to heat almost all the homes in the nation's capital, Reykjavik.

Geo-electricity

Just like other energy sources, geothermal hot water and steam can be used to drive turbines connected to electric generators. The world's biggest series of geothermal power plants is found in a region of California called the Geysers. There are 21 power plants using steam from more than 350 geothermal wells.

Is geothermal power available everywhere?

Some regions of the world are naturally much better suited than others to produce large-scale geothermal power. The availability of underground heat depends on the geological conditions of a location. Areas with volcanoes are generally very good. However, smaller-scale devices, such as heat pumps, can be used almost anywhere. Also, new technology is being developed that can tap into heat much deeper beneath the surface. One system, the Hot Dry Rock (HDR) system pumps water deep underground to heat up before being returned to the surface. In some countries, the siting of geothermal plants in national parks and other places of scenic interest is controversial and divides public opinion.

LEADING COUNTRIES PRODUCING GEO-ELECTRICITY

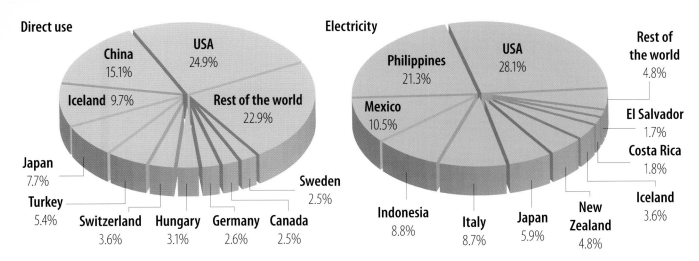

Direct use: USA 24.9%, Rest of the world 22.9%, China 15.1%, Iceland 9.7%, Japan 7.7%, Turkey 5.4%, Switzerland 3.6%, Hungary 3.1%, Germany 2.6%, Canada 2.5%, Sweden 2.5%

Electricity: USA 28.1%, Philippines 21.3%, Mexico 10.5%, Indonesia 8.8%, Italy 8.7%, Japan 5.9%, New Zealand 4.8%, Rest of the world 4.8%, Iceland 3.6%, Costa Rica 1.8%, El Salvador 1.7%

Small-scale heat pumps

The top few metres of the Earth's surface stay at a relatively constant temperature all year round. The ground is generally warmer than the air above it during winter, remaining at about 10-16°C. A geothermal heat pump takes advantage of this source of warmth by transferring it into a building.

What does the future hold?

The biggest challenge facing the world's energy industries is to keep up or increase power supplies without causing further global warming. Experts predict that the world's energy needs will grow by 55 per cent between 2005 and 2030. Demand for electricity is expected to double. Three quarters of the energy increase will be needed to supply developing countries.

The greenhouse effect

The biggest disadvantage (and the largest issue) surrounding fossil fuels is the way in which burning them adds to the greenhouse effect. The atmosphere prevents some of the Sun's rays from reaching Earth. Its gases also stop some heat escaping from Earth, just as glass traps warmth inside a greenhouse. We add to this natural greenhouse effect by emitting waste gases from power plants, factories and cars. Many greenhouse gases – especially carbon dioxide – are produced when we burn fossil fuels. That is why environmentalists favour renewable sources of energy, which emit very little or no greenhouse gas.

A rise in sea level would flood the world's low-lying islands, such as the Maldives in the Indian Ocean. This is one of the catastrophic effects that could be caused by global warming.

Adding to global warming

Scientists call the extra effect caused by human actions the enhanced greenhouse effect. This is of great concern because of the way in which global warming is changing our world. The 2007 report by the UN's Intergovernmental Panel on Climate Change (IPCC) reported that:

• world temperatures could rise by between 1.1 and 6.4°C during the twenty-first century;

• sea levels will probably rise by 18 to 59 cm by 2100;

• it is very probable (90 per cent certain) that there will be more frequent heatwaves and heavy rainfall;

• it is very likely (66 per cent certain) that there will be more droughts and hurricanes.

According to the IPCC's 2007 report: 'The primary source of the increased atmospheric concentration of carbon dioxide since the pre-industrial period results from fossil fuel use.'

THE WORLD'S BIGGEST CO_2 EMITTERS

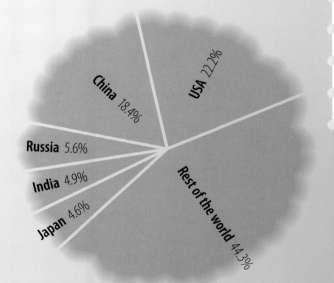

China 18.4%
USA 22.2%
Russia 5.6%
India 4.9%
Japan 4.6%
Rest of the world 44.3%

Shares of CO₂

Burning coal and oil currently releases more than three quarters of CO_2 emissions from power plants. The figures are as follows:

Coal	40.5 per cent
Oil	39.5 per cent
Natural gas	19.7 per cent
Others	0.3 per cent

Are the problems exaggerated?

Some people think that scientists may be exaggerating the effects of human-caused global warming. There have even been books and television programmes claiming this. Environmentalists call the disbelievers climate-change deniers. You have to form your own opinion, but bear in mind that the IPCC is a scientific body established by the World Meteorological Organization and the United Nations Environment Programme, with experts from more than 130 countries and more than 2500 scientific reviewers. The organization shared the 2007 Nobel Peace Prize with Al Gore (who made the Oscar-winning documentary film *An Inconvenient Truth*). The IPCC say that there is a five per cent chance (or 1 in 20) that any of their findings or conclusions could be wrong.

At the moment five countries produce more than half the world's total emissions.

Carbon dioxide per person

The amount of CO_2 emitted per person varies enormously around the world. By 2030 an average Chinese person is expected to be responsible for nearly twice as much CO_2 as he or she is today. But this will still be little more than a third of the CO_2 emitted by an average American.

Like all the world's cities, Melbourne in Australia is lit up by electricity at night.

Solar cities

The International Solar Energy Society (ISES) works to support the science of solar energy and research to show how it can be helpful here on Earth. One of its programmes is called the Solar Cities Initiative, which aims to look at the best ways to use energy in the 'habitats of tomorrow'. Scientists at ISES are particularly interested in cities as complete systems in themselves, where solar power could provide most energy.

TONNES OF CO₂ EMITTED PER PERSON

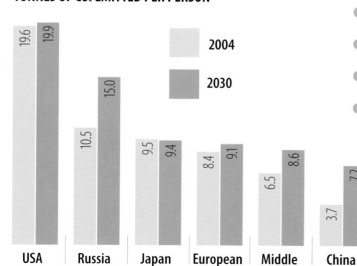

2004
2030

	2004	2030
USA	19.6	19.9
Russia	10.5	15.0
Japan	9.5	9.4
European Union	8.4	9.1
Middle East	6.5	8.6
China	3.7	7.2
Brazil	1.8	2.3
India	1.0	1.8
Africa	0.9	1.0
Rest of the world	3.3	3.9
World	4.1	5.0

Could we capture carbon?

Some experts consider carbon capture and storage (CCS) to be an important development. The process stops carbon dioxide from entering the atmosphere by removing it and storing it deep underground. The CO_2 can be removed before being burned by a method called gasification. Alternatively, it can be removed during the exhaust process at a power plant by absorbing it into a solvent. A third possibility is to burn the fuel in oxygen instead of air, which creates a stream of CO_2 that can be removed. The CO_2 separated by all these methods can be piped underground – into disused coalfields, rocks saturated with salt water or oil pockets.

What will the energy be used for?

Experts predict transport and industry will take an even greater share of energy in future. These are their predictions for energy consumption.

	2004 % share	2030 % share
Homes and agriculture	38.0	36.2
Industry	32.8	33.7
Transport	25.8	26.7
Other	3.4	3.4

The greatest recent growth in transport has been in air travel, and this rise is expected to continue.

Fossil fuel for flight

Jet aircraft burn a refined form of petroleum called kerosene. Some jets are powered by a mixture of gasoline, kerosene and other fuels. As air travel has increased, the quantity of jet fuel consumed has also increased enormously. The United States produces about 27 million barrels of kerosene and 435 million barrels of kerosene-type jet fuels each year. This makes up about a sixth of total US oil production. The worldwide figure will continue to go up because the number of air passengers is increasing by about six per cent per year. In 2006 there were 4.4 billion passenger flights worldwide, and this figure could more than double by 2020.

Will new energy sources be discovered?

It is impossible to answer this, but researchers are working on new sources, as well as on ways of using existing sources more efficiently. They are also trying to find cleaner, greener methods of burning fossil fuels. One possible future source might be nuclear fusion. Instead of splitting nuclei, they could be fused (or joined together) to create energy. Nuclear fusion devices are still at an experimental stage. Engineers have built several test reactors, but so far they have not proved practical. In 2006 China, the European Union, India, Japan, Russia, South Korea and the USA agreed to work together to fund a nuclear fusion project based in France. The US Department of Energy also has a special Fusion Energy Sciences Program.

Futuristic fuel cells

Another possibility for the future is the fuel cell. Just like electric generators, fuel cells convert chemical energy to electrical energy. One of the most useful kinds of fuel cell generates electricity by combining hydrogen (H) and oxygen (O), which then form water (H_2O). As the electricity is produced, water is given off as a harmless waste product, and this is one of the reasons why environmentalists are very keen on this technology. So long as it is supplied with the two gases, a fuel cell will go on producing electricity. Air is easily available as the source of oxygen, but hydrogen is not so easy to supply. Hydrogen is not an energy source, because we always need energy to produce it, but it is very useful as a carrier of energy. Other energy sources can be used to produce hydrogen, including biomass.

Saving energy

We can all contribute towards the world's future energy needs by using less energy. If everyone makes a small effort, it can amount to a large saving. In this way we can all lessen our contribution to the energy problem and increase our contribution to the solution. One of the easiest ways to do this is to use less electricity, which is especially important since most electricity is produced by burning fossil fuels. We can turn off lights and electrical equipment when they are not needed, including standby devices. We can also choose energy-efficient appliances, including low-energy, long-life light bulbs.

Cycling and recycling

We use an enormous amount of fuel for transport. In future, people may increasingly ask themselves whether they should walk or cycle (using the energy of their own muscles) to school or work, rather than going by car (using up precious fuel). Another way to save energy is to recycle as much material as possible, since it takes much less energy to recycle goods – glass, plastic, paper – than to make them from scratch.

In the rich countries of the world, most people throw away a sackful of rubbish every ten days. The sack often contains many items that could be recycled. We could also cut down on waste by using less in the first place. For example, we could use less packaging. We could buy food sold loose, rather than wrapped in plastic and packed on a tray.

Plastic bottles are recycled at this plant. The plastic is crushed, melted and remoulded into new containers.

What will the future energy mix be?

The energy mix may vary enormously in different countries. Overall throughout the world, by 2030 it will probably be similar to the prediction made by the International Energy Agency (see page 7). People who are very concerned about the environment and the effects of global warming would prefer to see renewable energy sources make up a much greater share of the mix. Those who worry more about an energy gap might want to continue with fossil fuels so long as they are available and affordable. People's attitudes to the contribution of nuclear power to the mix also vary enormously, depending on how they view the potential dangers. Now that you have read about the various sources and the issues surrounding them, what do you think?

Glossary

atom   The basic particle of all matter.

butane   A highly flammable gas present in oil and natural gas.

carbon   A non-metallic chemical element that occurs in coal and many other substances.

carbon dioxide (CO_2)   A greenhouse gas given off when fossil fuels are burned.

continental shelf   The sloping underwater area near land at the edge of a continent.

crude oil   Oil (or petroleum) as it is found naturally underground.

electron   A negatively charged particle within an atom.

emissions   Producing and giving off something (such as a waste gas); also, the waste gas produced and given off.

ethane   A highly flammable gas present in oil and natural gas.

ethanol (or ethyl alcohol)   A liquid biofuel that can be produced from plants such as sugar cane and maize.

fission   Splitting an atomic nucleus.

fossil fuel   A fuel (such as coal, oil and natural gas) that comes from the remains of prehistoric plants and animals.

fusion   Joining together of atomic nuclei.

generator   A machine that turns mechanical energy into electrical energy.

global warming   Heating up of the Earth's surface, especially caused by pollution from burning fossil fuels.

greenhouse gas   A gas, such as carbon dioxide, that traps heat from the Sun near the Earth and helps to create the greenhouse effect.

habitat   The natural home or environment of an animal or a plant.

hydrocarbon   A chemical compound containing hydrogen and carbon.

hydrogen   A light, colourless gas that combines with oxygen to make water.

kerogen   A tarry substance that is found in oil shale.

methane   A flammable gas that forms when organic matter decays; it is the main element of natural gas.

national electricity grid   A country's network of electric power lines.

non-renewable resources   Resources (such as fossil fuels) that are used up and cannot be replaced.

nucleus (plural **nuclei**)   The central part of an atom.

OPEC   The Organization of Petroleum [or Oil] Exporting Countries.

oxygen   A colourless gas that humans and animals need to breathe to live.

propane   A highly flammable gas present in oil and natural gas.

radioactive   Describing a substance such as uranium that has unstable atoms that give off energy in the form of streams of particles.

renewable energy sources   Sources of energy that do not run out, such as biomass, geothermal, solar, water and wind power.

turbine   A machine with rotating blades that turn a shaft.

ultraviolet rays   Electromagnetic rays with a shorter wavelength than visible light rays.

Websites

The US National Oceanic and Atmospheric Administration answers questions on greenhouse gases
http://lwf.ncdc.noaa.gov/oa/climate/gases.html#wv

The World Nuclear Association's view of the nuclear debate and safety
www.world-nuclear.org/info/inf06.htm

The International Geothermal Association (IGA) offers facts and data
http://iga.igg.cnr.it

The International Solar Energy Society – a global alliance
www.ises.org

The World Wind Energy Association on turbine history and technology
www.world-wind-energy.info

The benefits of biomass from the US National Renewable Energy Lab
www.nrel.gov/learning/re_biomass.html

Index